Published by Sellers Publishing, Inc.

Illustrations © 2014 Dave Coverly

Design by George Corsillo, Design Monsters

Sellers Publishing, Inc.

161 John Roberts Road, South Portland, Maine 04106

Visit our Web site sellerspublishing.com

E-mail: rsp@rsvp.com

ISBN 13: 978-1-4162-4509-4

10 9 8 7 6 5 4 3 2 1

Printed and bound in China

LAUGHTER IS THE BEST MEDICINE

DAVE COVERLY

Creator of

SPEED BUMP

SELLERS
PUBLISHING

Rx:

THE OFFICE VISIT

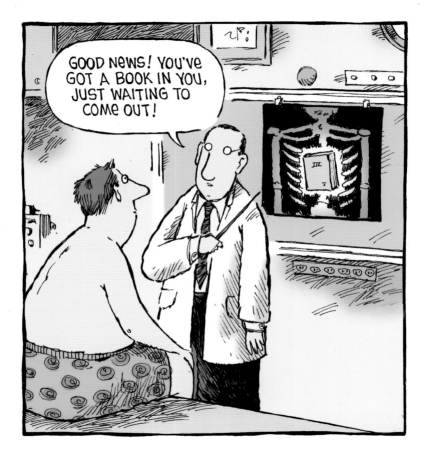

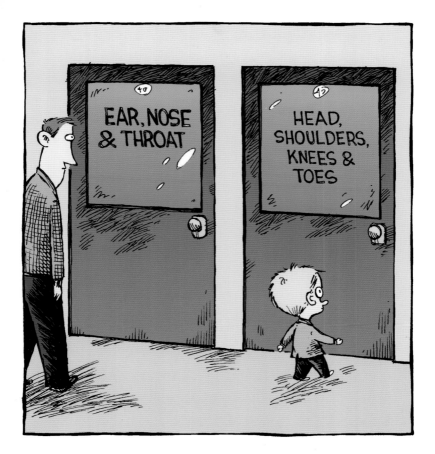

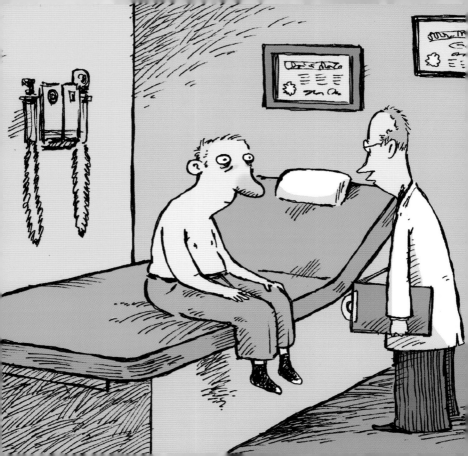

Rx:

IN THE HOSPITAL

eye test for pharmacists

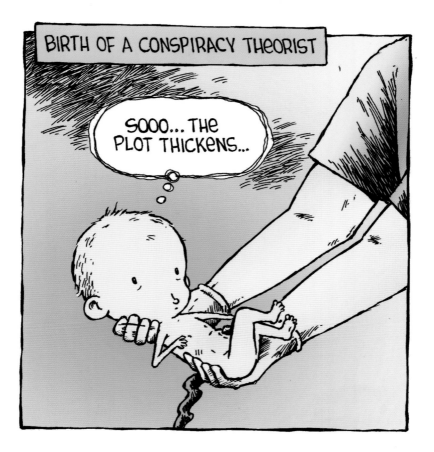

Rx:

IN
SURGERY